PERSONAL EXCELLENCE

By
Rev. Dr. Ray W. Lincoln

Copyright 2006, printed in New Zealand.

Copyright 2008, printed in the United States of America.

Copyright 2009, printed in the United States of America.

Copyright 2020, printed in the United States of America.

ISBN: 978-0-9996349-3-6

Dedication

To the few, but the outstanding, contributors to my life, who by their pursuit of great things inspired me to greater desires, and hence to a life much better than I was destined to live.

Thank you!

Acknowledgements

Many books on excellence have been instrumental in forming my thoughts and my life. To acknowledge all of them would take a book of its own.

Some have been a form of shock treatment — their pointed words, a way into a heart hard to penetrate. I cannot but be grateful for all they taught me by this method.

Others have softly informed and nurtured me on a mental path that enriched my passage.

No one book confines itself to a single method because the reader detects firm handedness and tactful approach differently. All must write with the passion that drives them and this, as I look back, is the thing that made each so meaningful to me — truth with passion.

Without passion why do we write? Books are truth, delivered through personality, expressed on the page and interpreted by the reader through his own personality. Therefore, I acknowledge all my sources of knowledge and personal change with a hope. That hope is that this small contribution to the search for personal excellence will, somehow at least, achieve the arousal of passions to that end in all my readers' minds.

One book, the Bible, has far outstripped the others in the formation of my life. This is what I expected. It has done the same for countless millions.

Thanks to my wife for her willing, loving efforts at making the manuscript better than the draft I handed her.

Contents

PERSONAL EXCELLENCE

How to proceed

I offer these principles as a starting place for all those who would seek excellence.

By keeping the length of this booklet brief it can easily be read in one sitting by even a busy person.

After reading it through, I would suggest that you take one principle each day and mentally digest the thoughts presented and the creative reactions of your own mind to what is written. Your thoughts that arise from my words are of great importance and should not be lost. Therefore, jot down your thoughts, determinations, ideas and inspirations for careful consideration in the forming of your pathway to excellence.

For the best impact on your mind and life, approach the reading of this book with a high level of excitement. You are about to discover things that will determine the success of your life.

Good findings and God bless.

Introduction

Jesus was excellence personified. When He made wine, He made the best; when He loved, He loved without restraint; His teachings go unsurpassed over two millennia; His leadership cannot be faulted; He lived without sin or wrong; He paid in full whatever price His cause demanded; His mind was brilliant and His emotions were controlled to perfection.

We are His followers. Excellence, too, must be our pursuit in all things. He sets our sights as high as His own: "Be perfect as your Heavenly Father is perfect."

Excellence is always aiming to be better, always "pressing toward the mark." If this makes some souls tighten with anxiety and pressure, perhaps they have mistaken the path to excellence with a road called "You'd better shape up" or "You're not good enough."

To others whose aimless wander has been a silent poem to procrastination, Jesus' call to perfection may feel like the callous imposition of a guilt trip. Would a skilled motivator like Jesus confuse negative threats with the inspiration of a beckoning summit?

Of course not! He is calling us to the discovery of our potential and the promise of His comforting presence along the way. He leads by love and grace. To be caught in the up-draught of His love is to be rediscovered and remade. It is exciting! Follow His call.

In search of excellence we need to build into our life habits that are the supporting structure for excellent behavior. The following eleven principles are not exhaustive, but a selection of actions we cannot do without. So start now and make them, one-by-one, automatic patterns in your lifestyle.

Habits… are the supporting structure for excellent behavior.

There isn't a personality created by the all-wise God that doesn't find personal fulfillment in the results that these principles implant.

The following "helps" to excellence are the inevitable out-workings of a disciplined life full of faith.

Principle One: "Seek first the Kingdom of God and His righteousness."

Excellence begins with our relationship to God and ends in a life mature, full of good and satisfying works, displaying the image of the One who created us. Excellence means looking like the God who made us.

Mould your life according to the shape of your Creator

Excellence is not just moral excellence, but excellence in all things God-like. God is a God of order, says Paul, as well as a God of love. Order is God-like. We may express it in different ways. My desk may not be as neat as you may think it has to be, but its filing system is order to me. When my mind is ordered, I am orderly. Don't impose your systems on me, I ask; but impose the values of God's character. The values that mark that character and achievement should be everyone's passionate aim. Express them as you must.

The overall character of God is described as righteousness in more places in the Bible than I wish to count. The Greek word it uses for righteousness is really the word for "right-ness." It is derived from the Greek word "dike" (instructress), which was also the name for the daughter of Zeus, who was seen to be involved in the government of the world. "Government," "righteousness" — the words seem to be unlikely bedfellows! But in Greek mythology it came to mean "doing what was fitting and right."

9

So, to be righteous is to behave in a manner that fits the Kingdom of God. Hence it includes all good — love as opposed to hate; order as opposed to disorder; achievement as opposed to failure; good as opposed to evil; faith as opposed to unbelief.

Set your sights on all that fits the Kingdom of God. Mould your life according to the shape of your Creator. Seek that outline of excellence with all your heart.

Principle Two: Always have a goal.

This is by no means a surprise. In fact, people have always known this. Among the ancient sayings recorded in the book of Proverbs is this similar gem of wisdom: *"Without a vision the people perish." (Proverbs 29:18).* A vision is a dream, a goal; something that sharpens our focus and calls us into the future with purpose. A goal is a defined purpose. Never leave home without one!

A goal is a defined purpose.

It all makes sense. A boat charts a course and to do so must determine a destination. An aircraft submits a flight plan. A builder first draws up the plans and follows his blueprint. Hudson Taylor, one of the world's most adventuresome missionaries, had a goal: China for Christ. He did not achieve his goal in his lifetime, but it defined all he did; and without it, perhaps, he would have achieved little. Achievement by definition requires a measure, a point at which it can be said to have been reached. The measure — the goal — determines the achievement.

Is your life defined by a goal?
Have you written it down?
Or is your life a happening moulded by whatever forces blow
you around?

Is your life defined by a goal? Have you written it down? Or is your life a happening moulded by whatever forces blow you around? And worse, are

11

you a meandering menace — a threat to the safety of others on the highway of life? Jesus had a goal. That's good enough for me. *"He set His face as a flint toward the cross" and* would not be turned aside by tempting shortcuts to earthly glory.

It not only marked for us when He arrived at the goal of His earthly life, but it focused His mind and His powers. "He set his face as a flint" — its cutting edge was razor sharp to his mind.

Goals that are blunt-faced or fuzzy are not goals; they are not even general directions. I would not want to board a plane that listed as its flight plan "Somewhere up there." Goals must be precise and indelibly written on paper and heart. Goals motivate. A general direction is hardly inspiring.

When encouraging His disciples after telling them that He would be leaving them, He said that they would be where He was. It is not enough to know that our eternal meeting place is somewhere inside or outside this vast universe. But it is deeply satisfying to know it is where He is. We want to go there because we know the exact place where we are going. It is where we want to be. The more definitive the goal the more motivation it provides.

The Bible's message is all about goals — God's goals — His goals for us; our goals to personal satisfaction and salvation. Therefore, we should have a passion to be goal-oriented people.

This is not a treatise on goal-setting. If you don't know how to set good goals, it is a call to attend a goal-setting seminar or gain the experience necessary to make defining, achievable-with-a-stretch, exciting goals.

The more definitive the goal,
the more motivation it provides.

Principle Three: Always have a plan to reach your goal.

Watching people through the years has convinced me of this: If you don't have a plan you're all talk. And, since talk is cheap and demands nothing more than the expiring of a little hot air, real commitment (the food of champions) is not your breakfast.

Jesus had a plan, and even a schedule for His plan. He often said, *"My hour is not yet come," and* therefore, refusing to receive the people's acclaim that would speed up their plans for Him. He knew what was next and when it should happen. He stuck to His plan.

A plan contains: (1) the steps needed to reach the goal; (2) the methods that you will use to reach that goal; and (3) the schedule for its achievement. Anything that does not contain these three ingredients is an incomplete plan. People who succeed don't begin building with incomplete blueprints.

A plan requires that you think through your goal with analytical skills and the necessary details so as to count the cost, purchase the materials and hire the necessary help. A plan must include how, when and why we are going to enlist the help of others in its achievement — a how, when and why for everything. I know it is tedious to make a detailed plan. That's why I have often succumbed to the temptation that I can "wing it" (make it up as I went along). However,

14

consider the foolishness of winging the most important thing you will ever build: your life.

A well written plan is a job half done.

So, knuckle down to the details. Our memories were not intended to be our blueprints. The plan in its details must be written down! In written form it can be scrutinized for redundancies, errors, weaknesses and inadequacies. A well written plan is a job half done.

A plan contains:
(1) The steps needed to reach the goal;
(2) The methods that you will use to reach that goal; and
(3) The schedule for its achievement.

Go over your plan at regular, predetermined intervals and change what needs to be changed. A good plan has the flexibility to alter its path to the goal because unforeseen events will require new approaches or new materials. But never does a good plan allow for the altering of the goal itself, — particularly the lessening of the goal so that we can opt out when the struggle becomes too tough.

Any good book or seminar on goal-setting will help you learn the science of planning. Invest in one.

Principle Four: Manage your time before others manage it for you.

And they will! People are experts at using other people's time while being poor managers of their own. People want us to do things for them. Then, if they fail, we — not them — can be blamed. I am not meaning to be harsh, but rather to provoke us to self-management. It's your life. Don't let anyone manage it for you. Other people will not be held responsible for our lives. We will!

It's your life. Don't let anyone manage it for you.

A plan needs time to make it work, and hence the need for time management. We live in a space/time environment. We are limited by both. To maximize the benefit of time we must plan its use. A schedule is a must, even if it is sketchy. It comprises the listing of events and tasks with a time allocation and a definite time slot for each task and event. Priorities are the rules that govern good time management. All tasks and events fall into one of four categories.

1. **High Importance/High Urgency.** These items must be attacked first. They head your list for today!
2. **High Importance/Low Urgency.** These are next and should be scheduled into your calendar for completion in the near future.
3. **Low Importance/High Urgency.** Because of the urgency, find shortcuts to get these done with little

or no personal involvement. Delegate them if at all possible.

4. **Low Importance/Low Urgency.** Do you really have to do these? Can someone else do them? Do they really have to be done at all? At times when something has to be left undone these are the first to go. To avoid embarrassment, review these items periodically. They can become more urgent or more important; and then they should be re-categorized as a (3) or even a (2).

I suggest this system because it assigns each task or event a place on your schedule based on both importance and urgency. At times, urgency can trump importance; but importance is far more determinative of a task's worth than simple urgency. It could be urgent for me to write a report; but, if someone else can write it for me to read and sign, I can be relieved for a task that only I can do.

Most people do things based on how urgent they are. They leave things until they are urgent enough to demand their attention. Important tasks as a result can be left undone simply because they are not demanding that they be done right now.

Priority is made up of both importance and urgency. Get into the habit of thinking about all the things you must do in terms of both.

Find a good calendar — either hard copy or software — and always keep it updated. Schedule all of your tasks by the above ranking and label them "1, 2, 3, or 4".

Priority is made up of both importance and urgency.

One final thought. The Bible talks about redeeming the time, (Ephesians 5:16). To redeem means "to buy back." Sometimes, when an important item is missed, you will have to buy back the time you need to do it by sacrificing something else. To buy back the time, your need to do important things is always the wise thing to do.

How do I buy time back? Buy back time that you lost by delegating less important things on your list to other people. Alternatively, if it is unimportant, simply don't do it. This way, you have time to do something you really need to do and your work is made more effective.

The Bible's term for time management is stewardship. We are stewards of all that God gave us. God gave us time.

Learn to manage your own time!

Principle Five: Get the action habit.

Action requires effort to get a task "off the ground." Everything remains in a state of rest or the motion of equalized force unless it is propelled upward to a new level by some energy. Inertia must be overcome in order to make progress. Only action can create the movement you need.

The person who is always "getting ready to" live life to its fullest confuses living with dying. "I'm about to...," "I'm waiting for...," "Tomorrow..." "When I'm up to it...," and like statements are phrases that usually betray a lack of energizing resolve.

The person who is always "getting ready to" live life to its fullest confuses living with dying.

Why spend years in silent hurt when all that stood in the way of success was getting started? It hurts when, late in life, we realize what we could have done if only we were purposefully active.

Fear at the starting gate is greater than fear in the heat of the race. When the adrenalin rushes through our veins, we are empowered and we focus more urgently on the immediate task. We get more done in a shorter time frame. If you can overcome fear at the start, nothing should be able to stop you.

A problem is not something that must be overcome before we start, but an obstacle that is only demolished as our will, already on the move, presses
19

over it. Action is all a matter of will. Problems are often not solved before action is taken. It's in the path to their solution that the answer appears.

If you can overcome fear at the start,
nothing should be able to stop you.

You haven't started because you are afraid of making a mistake? You are making the biggest mistake! Fight procrastination because it is a thief. It makes today unproductive and crowds tomorrow. "One day's trouble is enough for the day," (Matthew 6:34). Know your priorities and take action on them daily.

An excellent book on identifying and overcoming procrastination is: *"Procrastination, Why You Do It and What to Do About It,"* by Jane B. Burka, Ph.D., and Lenora M. Yuen, Ph.D.

Fight procrastination because it is a thief.
It makes today unproductive and
crowds tomorrow.

Principle Six: Never quit.

Sir Winston Churchill once gave an address at his alma mater using only two words, "Never, Never, Never quit!" That was all he said; and then —to the surprise of all — he sat down.   Would it be remembered? Did it say enough? I think so.

Luke 9:62 records the words of Jesus, *"No man having put his hand to the plow and turning back is fit for the Kingdom of God."* There is a disqualifying clause in this statement that is designed to motivate us, not to de-motivate us.

But, however you feel about being termed unfit for God's kingdom, to quit surely questions our commitment in the first place.

The temptation to quit is fierce in the face of adversity and loss.

The temptation to quit is fierce in the face of adversity and loss. I must confess that at times in my journey I have contemplated the benefits of just dropping out of life and hiding. But "when the road becomes tough, the tough keep going." Those words have kept me at the grind more times than I can remember.

Life is queer with its twists and turns,
As every one of us sometime learns;
And many a failure turns about,
When he might have won had he stuck it out.

21

Don't give in though the race seems slow.
You may succeed with another blow.
Success is failure turned inside out,
The silver tint of the clouds of doubt;
And you never can tell how close you are;
It may be near when it seems so far.
So stick to the fight when you're hardest hit.
It's when things seem worse
That you must not quit.

Author Unknown

The surest way not to fail is to determine to succeed.

Principle Seven: Never give excuses.

Once again, as in every principle in this booklet, the point is made by Jesus either in His teaching or His life. He told a parable of those who were invited to a wedding feast — a *feast,* mind you — and they all began to make excuses (Luke 14:16-24). What is it with us, that we are more prone to making excuses than we are to grasping opportunities? The excuses were absurd into the bargain. One man said he had bought a piece of land and had to go and see it!

Anyone in their right mind would look at the land before they bought it, wouldn't you think? I question this person's business acumen.   Another said he "married a wife and can't come." What wife would turn down a banquet? This was clearly not his wife's decision.

Escaping the opportunities of life, for those who are allergic to challenges, becomes a way of life that is more like a way of death.

An excuse is nothing but a way out. A way out is an escape — a way to bypass an offer, opportunity or obligation.   Escaping the opportunities of life, for those who are allergic to challenges, becomes a way of life that is more like a way of death.

We could benefit from the advice, "Don't keep constant company with those who are always making excuses." The disease is all too easily caught.

Excuses kill unexpected opportunities. A person who pursues excellence lives with all antennas raised for whatever might be — just might be — coming their way.

Excuses kill unexpected opportunities.

Excuses betray a psychological disease variously diagnosed as fear, laziness, depression and aimlessness (excuse the more meaningful lay terms). We must learn to examine ourselves when we find ourselves giving excuses. Perhaps we can excuse ourselves, but only when something more important is knocking on our door.

Principle Eight: Never criticize or grumble.

Again, Jesus said it more effectively: *"Do not judge lest you be judged," (Matthew 7:1).*   Perhaps His most arresting comment on the subject was, *"How can you say to your brother, 'Let me take the speck out of your eye,' when all the time there is a plank in your own eye?" (Matthew 7:4).*   The critic often holds up a mirror revealing himself.

- To criticize is to declare that we have nothing better to do.
- To criticize is to judge others — an occupation that does not belong to mortals.
- To criticize is to waste our time when time is the more valuable commodity.
- To criticize is to open ourselves to criticism.   Any takers?
- To criticize is to engage in a negative task that gives birth to negative forces.   Negative forces in our lives are damaging.
- To criticize is to display a sense of pride.
- To criticize is to be blind to our own faults, or to minimize them.
- To criticize is to invite the judgment of God.
- To criticize is to find company.   Do you want the company you have found?

When we find ourselves criticizing along with others who criticize we have lost our edge.   Christ never grumbled; but He had it rough.   Take a look at the cross again!   Long-suffering, such as He displayed, is the fruit of God's Spirit and it is shortened and neutralized by grumbling.

The critic often holds up a mirror revealing himself.

A negative power is generated by negative talk. The way of excellence leads off in the other direction: uplifting, positive talk.

Principle Nine: Remember, attitudes are more important than facts.

If all the facts are against us, attitude is our trump card.   Don't let the facts distract you if you know what God would have you do.   Facts are rearranged and revalued by faith.   They lose their negative qualities because of faith.   This is the attitude that triumphs over the seemingly impossible.

Remember that attitudes are made up of beliefs. Beliefs are the motivating factors in our minds and lives.

If all the facts are against us, attitude is our trump card.

When God created the universe, it is said that He created it out of nothing by faith.   The facts were lined up against Him.   How can you create something out of nothing?   How can matter or energy be made out of nothing?   And perhaps even more puzzling for us humans is the concept that something can be made by faith alone.

Creative faith (belief) is the raw material of attitudes, and the belief and the resultant attitude can be good or bad.   Either way, our attitudes will empower us and create the results they predict.   The question becomes: What results do we want to create and with what velocity do we wish to propel them into our lives?

Our attitudes will reproduce themselves — and they will do so to the intensity we believe in them. The life of faith is not the life of facts. Faith — not facts — is our daily challenge.

It all boils down to living by the unseen qualities of life. Pay attention to the tangible and logical, but make the spiritual more important. Only faith is there to lead us when the path ahead is unknown and dark. Our positive attitude unlocks the spiritual forces and releases their power.

Principle Ten: Always accept full responsibility. Don't pass the buck!

Phrases, such as those below, which typify our lack of willingness to take responsibility, litter our language.

"The devil made me do it!"

"My wife is responsible…"

"Well, if you had a mother like mine, you, too, would…"

"What else can you expect with a no good husband like mine?"

"He made me mad."

"It's not my fault."

Each of these dismissals of personal responsibility thinly hides the spirit of a coward. It takes courage to face up to our beliefs, attitudes, thoughts and actions and change them where needed. A humble spirit is one that always knows the possibility that we could be wrong. Always be willing to admit wrong, even potential wrong.   It doesn't weaken a person of conviction for them to be cautious about their own abilities or knowledge.

Accept the responsibility for the results of your own actions. Reconciliation — the spirit that declares a willingness to make things right and the actions to accomplish it — is simply an indication of personal integrity.

Better to accept responsibility for what we have not done than not to accept responsibility for what we have done. Jesus reminded all of us (who skillfully pass the buck), "Everyone shall give an account of himself to God." Wow!

Excuses are not the way of excellence. Excuses are the breakfast, lunch and dinner of losers.

*Better to accept responsibility for what we have not done
than not to accept responsibility
for what we have done.*

Principle Eleven: Work smart.

Multiply yourself through others. When we share, give ourselves away to others, teach others, lead others, and influence others, we multiply ourselves for good or for bad. There seems to be no law of addition in the spiritual life. Everything multiplies once it has been given life in a human thought or action.

Everything multiplies
once it has been given life
in a human thought or action.

Leverage your time, money and influence. Invest for great gains. Save, and you only fall behind the rising cost of living. I don't mean just money! Invest in the quality of your life! Quality comes at the cost of living well.

Remember the 20/80 rule:

- Twenty percent of the people do eighty percent of the work.
- Twenty percent of the people take eighty percent of the responsibility.
- Twenty percent of the people possess eighty percent of the reward.

The way of excellence belongs to the "twenty per-centers."

Also remember: When you are the anvil, bear; when you are the hammer, strike!

We began with the thought that Jesus was excellence personified and that we are His followers. Why not start your path to excellence by reading one of the four books on the life of Jesus. They are the gospels Mathew, Mark, Luke and John — all contained in the Bible. Ignorance of who Jesus really is, what he taught and what he did, is not an excuse for not benefiting from His wisdom.

Read to discover example after example of how He did in fact personify these principles. Read to take on board the power of His words. Digest His life for the challenge He gave us — a challenge few have taken and only those of excellence can say they have at least partially explored.

Choose one of the above principles, one at a time, and make it your own.

About the Author

Ray Lincoln has served as senior pastor to single and multi-staffed churches in New Zealand, Australia and the USA. His 40 plus years of experience in coaching, counseling and teaching have given him the opportunity to guide many people to self-discovery and spiritual renewal. He has studied extensively in the areas of Temperament/Psychology, Theology, Philosophy and Neuroscience and has earned a BA, BD, MDiv, PhD and LTh.

Teaching people to succeed in life and overcome their challenges with God's strength are his passion. Ray says, "While remaining true to the teachings of the Christian tradition, my strong interest has been to use the best of science and develop a true Christian Psychology that can help people find true fulfillment. God wants this for all of us. He knows best how we function and has left us the most helpful life-manual in the best-selling book ever!"

Conducting hundreds of seminars in Australia, New Zealand and the USA has led him to lecture in universities, seminaries, and Bible colleges as well as businesses and churches. He has mentored pastors and other professionals. Ray offers his services, experience and knowledge to you. His wife, Mary Jo, is more than a willing partner in his ministry and, in her own right, contributes much to their joint mission.

www.ingramcontent.com/pod-product-compliance
Lightning Source LLC
Chambersburg PA
CBHW060554030426

42337CB00019B/3543